This book is not based on personal accounts from my own life.

I've divided this title into specific sections, so that you as the reader can go to the very issues that you may be currently dealing with/which may relate to you.

I've been writing poetry, since I was six years old, and my poetry has always been based upon the issues I was dealing with at the time if writing.

NOTE: The poetry included in the opening of every subject is meant to be pessimistic. The poetry in the closing is meant to be optimistic. Hopefully, you'll enjoy it.

In a world where one can feel like an outsider, and depression can easily lead to self-destruction, even suicide, I've created this work of art with the objective to assure those who suffer, they are not alone, because.... I Feel Your Pain...

Table Of Contents

Chapter: 1 Victim of Abuse

Chapter: 2 Dealing with depression

Chapter: 3 A Victim of Bullying

Chapter: 4 When You Feel Like It You
                   Against The World

Chapter: 5 Dealing With Drug Addicted Parents

Chapter: 6 Contemplating Suicide

Chapter: 7 No One To Trust

Chapter: 8 Being Your Own Worst Enemy

Chapter: 9 Trying To Find Yourself

…..VICTIM OF ABUSE….

Chapter # 1

When you think that no one can hear your cries, trust me… I heard you yesterday.

When the scars have healed and you think no one can see that you're hurt, trust me….
   I Feel Your Pain
      Sincerely, Awond

Quiet Screams

Behind closed doors, I suffer by the hands of someone beating and belittling me.

I know my physical wounds will heal. The everlasting ones appear to be emotionally.

This blood will be washed away. But these psychological scars... I'll forever carry with me.

These scars will be a third party... partnering with whoever chooses to marry me.

"Why?", I question, but never aloud. This, I whisper to God.

In public, I disguise my frown, with a smile. Boy, my joy is a mirage.

Who can I tell that I'm trapped in hell? Most don't care to listen.

I call to God. But, I'm still on call waiting. My issues don't receive much attention.

Some scars I can't hide, and with time, it's hard to produce logical explainations.

The people around me struggle to add it up, their strongest curriculum is not

calculations... based on these basics.

   Poem by. Awond

...Tough Times...

I Feel Your Pain

Young and defenseless,
I've become prey to the predator.
Held captive, this prison is a world of fear,
And these prison guards are never letting up.

My body is aching from vicious beatings,
My dingy clothes cover my fresh wounds.
I can never relax after such attacks, as I
Know they'll be more attacks coming soon.

Trapped in a cycle of pain,
My tears resemble the rain.
The difference is that it'll never rain forever,
Yet these tears will forever flow across my face.
Poem by Awond

My Testimony...

When I was four years old, I was removed from the custody of my biological parents, due to allegations of abuse, neglect and my parents being addicted to drugs. Unfortunately, my foster mother turned out to be more abusive than both of my parents put together.

Failing to do a proper investigation, D.C.F.S placed my siblings and myself with a woman who had a history of having nervous breakdowns, being placed into mental institutions and being abusive to her own children. Without a question, this woman was unfit in every sense of the word.

My earliest memories regarding my childhood are full of mental and physical abuse. Being beaten, belittled, forced to sleep on the floor without blankets, bound and gagged in the basement was the daily routine for me. The smallest infraction would lead to me being beat with broomsticks, extension cords and metal poles. Despite growing up under these circumstances from the age of four, I was wise enough to know that my life was far from normal.

From day one, my siblings and I were told by our foster parent that we'd be killed, if we were to ever tell anyone about the way that we were being treated. Her threats were easy to believe, seeing that she nearly beat us to death on several occasions. There were times when she'd force my older sister and myself into the trunk of the car, and drive around, saying that she was looking for a place to dump our bodies, after she'd killed us. Fortunately, she never followed through with that plan.

For many years, we suffered in silence. I smiled in the face of the world, pretending as if my life was fine. I did my best to fit in with others, knowing that my life was too abnormal for others to relate to. So, I became a good actor. My pride also played a part in me not admitting that I was being abused and treated like an animal.

Around the time that I was eight years old, my siblings and I were removed from the custody of my foster mother and placed into protective custody. This was a result of my older sister telling someone at her school about the abuse that she was going through. On top of that, she had a broken arm as a result of a beating she endured under the care of our foster mother. So, we were removed from the home, while an investigation was taken place.

I saw the time away from my foster mother as an opportunity to tell my own story and possibly avoid being placed back in her custody, I corroborated my sister's story, and told the authorities my own experiences, including the death threats.

As a result of this ordeal, my foster mother was found guilty of neglect, abuse and mental cruelty. I was confident that at last this nightmare was over. I was wrong. While my older sister was permanently removed from my foster home, my younger siblings and I were returned to the same haunted house that we knew as home. Feeling betrayed and let down by the system, I went back to being silent, while the abuse continued, and got back to making up excuses for the scars I had. Throughout the years, I was extremely depressed, I had trouble sleeping and would often contemplate suicide.

After being abused for years, I questioned my self-worth. I questioned, why God would allow this to happen, and for the abuse to go on for so many years. Were my prayers and calls to God deemed unworthy of his attention? The pain caused from not having answers lasted longer than the physical pain ever would.

When I was 12 years old, I'd went to a school dance, against my foster mother's approval. After many years of being kept from having friends... being on sports teams, or even having friends, I was simply fed up. Hell, I wanted to experience some fun.

My foster mother was awaiting me, when I arrived at home. In a violent rage, she attacked me, striking me with a 14in metal pipe, until I fell to the floor in pain. Placing her foot on my neck, she continued to beat me, ignoring my muffled cries.

My foster mother struck me repeatedly, until she grew tired. Afterwards, she sent me to the basement, ordered me to strip, then tied me to a pole that ran from the ceiling to the floor, duct tape covered my mouth. For the next 24 hours, I stayed in the basement, deprived of food and only being untied to use the restroom. And, this was only another horrible day out of three years of torture.

* * *

I paid an expensive price for attending that particular school dance. But, within those few hours of being normal, my pride was born. I realized, I deserve to be happy, just as much as anyone else. I was determined to be set free. I began running away from home, every chance I could. Even though, I spent many nights homeless or in the juvenile detention center, I was safer and better off than if I was at home, most importantly it felt good to know that I was capable of removing myself out of a depressing situation, even if the alternatives were not ideal. At the age of 13, D.C.F.S ended up officially removing me from my foster home, placing me in a boy's home. But, by then, I was a young rebel, full of anger, fear and no trust nor respect for the system. Not knowing how to deal with my issues in a constructive way, I found myself on the path of self-destruction and being antisocial. Only now am I in the process of true healing, mentally and emotionally. But the process will be more than likely everlasting, as somethings are hard to forgive and remain to be water under the bridge. I'm obviously not happy about the abuse I endured at the hands of my foster home. I try not to drown in depression. Accepting the past, I utilize my experiences as my motivation to be successful and more understanding of others. For years, I was ordered to speak to psychologists, and to take psychiatric medication, in order to deal with my anger issues... sleep disorder and depression. I suffered from nightmares, flashbacks, paranoia, etc. I had severe trouble communicating and trusting others.

I believe that certain methods will work for certain people. But, personally, growing up, I had difficulties, buying into any solutions that book smart folks tried to sell me. No Dr. Phil can tell me how to deal with being bound and gagged as a kid, being beat until I was unconscious, starved daily, sleeping on the streets, etc. Individuals who haven't walked in my shoes couldn't relate to me.

So, within time, I stopped talking to all of those 'book smart folks and opted not to take the medications that were prescribed to me. Because I don't understand how drugs with serious side effects used to block out reality could ever be a permanent solution. Today, my philosophy is no rain equals no roses.

No rain equals no roses... all of those stars can't shine, when the sun is out, brightening up the day. Pride, courage and wisdom is a few of the things that'll make us overcome our adversity. Real stars shine the brightest, during the darkest times. And, in this sense, I'm determined to be a real star.

To anyone who's a victim of abuse, and is struggling to understand why, I believe it's because you're meant to be a star, by surviving and using your experiences to shine light upon others, when they're in the same darkness.

If you're currently being abused, have knowledge, faith and the confidence to walk away and seek help. Trust that you have the power to control your own destiny. Always remember that when you save yourself, you're a survivor. But, when you save someone else, you're a hero. Therefore, utilize your knowledge, experiences and strengths to relate to, and help others who experience similar circumstances, never let your pain rob you of peace and happiness.

Beautiful, you are

Accept the things that you cannot change, remember that the only thing you can't change is the past. When it rains, it pours… smiles drown in thunderstorms but at least float safely to shore, because this rain will never last.

Only the strong will survive in this world, and I know, these tough times makes you want to cry. But the knowledge that many can't walk a mile in your shoes should make you hold your head up with pride.

You see, life promises no smiles nor sun. Unfortunately, the only guarantee is death… So when you bring joy into your life, you've earned the feel good about yourself.

Accept the things that you cannot change. Don't carry any burdens into tomorrow. Today's the first day of the rest of your life. Don't live it drowning in sorrow.

No rain equals no roses. Without hard times, who would you be? Adversity is the essential tool, for building a beautiful person, on the outside and underneath.

Every authentic diamond in the world was discovered underneath the earth. Precious jewel's, buried beneath the surface. Thanks to the hard times, you're a star waiting to shine, as long as through this thunderstorm you float safe to shore.... Because I promise you no rain equals no roses.

Daily Thoughts...

Born into a world of sin, buried alive in the midst of adversity and pain... Tortured daily, like a slave, Stripped of my dignity, identity and my name.

I reached out to God, for his helping hand... begged for his guidance. But he never reached back, completing the connection. My calls were never acknowledged.

My cries went unheard, my tears shed, without being noticed. I often felt as if the dealer must've dealt me the cards that the other players never wanted.

My body's been covered with scars, from abuse which sounds unreal. The physical scars are mostly gone. But my mind and heart carries wounds that'll never heal.

There's nothing that I trust to make me better more than my pain. Because in order to rise from the dirt, even roses need some rain. Poem, by Awond.

DEALING WITH DEPRESSION.

Chapter #2

When you're sitting in that cold dark world, and you believe that there's no one who cares...

You're never alone.. you were never alone. You see I've been here, caring before you ever got here.

I Feel Your Pain...

By Awond

Gray clouds ...

raindrops resemble my tears, some people find the site of them falling relishing while others simply block them out, as the sun is shining in the real world, I'm being smothered by gray clouds.

Dark days, cold nights.... this depression is everlasting, a neve ending cycle. I hold on some hope for joy because doing these storms a faithful forecast is vital.

Some say "A change is coming ", but these tough times seems to be everlasting. if I could turn my frown into a smile, or these grey skies blue I suppose that would be an act of magic.

I Feel Your Pain

I am passionate about passing through these drastic days unscathed. But dear, I'm aware that pressure burst pipes. And, I cannot escape the weight of the world on my shoulders every day and night.

Crushing, like the Russians way back on Bloody Sunday, it's Tuesday and my soul's been crying for many years, I pray for joy to come someday.

I'm subordinate so my sadness, a slave to my own sorrow, while many is waiting for the sun to shine in the morning, my personal weather forecast predicts heavy rain, for tomorrow.

Poem, By Awond

Depressed...

My savior is faceless, I search, yet I never find... that tomorrow that's been promised to be a better day, instead worse days come aligned.

In time the lights may shine, and the truth may escape But, my clock is running behind. Therefore, the time may come too late.

This, I fear, in silence, never out loud. The truth never soars. It stays with me, like the pain in me, drowning me, behind closed doors.   Poem, By Awond.

In Pain... It feels as if no one speaks my language. Because they cannot relate to my pain. Within time, it feels like everyone is in on my abuse, this world is neglecting me every day.

Held captive in these chains, freedom is no friend of mine. Because even in society, my pain, my joy, and my peace remain confined.

My clothes cover my fresh wounds. My face carries a fake smile. While we are said to be living to die, I will die to live, right now.Yes, I'll die to live. Because death has to be better than life. Away from this World of Darkness, where even on sunny days, I see no light.

My Testimony ...

At 12 years old, I'd ran away from home, numerous of times, due to the abuse   that I was enduring. Then, one day, despite me telling the authorities about the abuse I was being subjected to, my caseworker what's driving me back to my foster home, after I'd just been released from the juvenile detention center. As soon as we pulled up in front of the house, I open the car door and took off running, disappearing instead of the night.

Without having a relationship with my biological family, and being prohibited from visiting friends, I'd been living a pretty isolated life. If I was to go to the police, I'd only been returned to juvie or my foster home. So, hours after running away, I found myself walking the streets, depressed about my situation. I felt trapped in a horrible nightmare. Then, to make matters worse, it started pouring down raining! I started to cry, my tears mixing with the raindrops.

I made it through last night and many similar ones, throughout my life. And, the hardest part was always feeling ask if I could not tell others about what I was going through. making up lies in wearing a fake smile was natural, but exhausting. it is the equivalent of putting makeup over scars. Though hidden to others, I know that those scars are there.

Anytime I was with my friends and hoping to be doing something fun, I was never able to fully enjoy the moment. the dark cloud of reality always hovered over me. I was 12 years old, trying to deal with being taken away from my parents, being abused, being away from my siblings, being homeless, yes at any minute capable of being in juvenile detention center or back in my foster home. And, all the while, I was trying to survive in the streets, while upholding a façade. Exhausting!!! I was struggling to maintain my sanity on the daily basis.

Due to my depression, and being diagnosed as mentally injured,

Awond Malone

I've spoken to many psychologists. I've been diagnosed with many different things and have been prescribed many different medications. Yet, through it all, my depression has remained, acting as my shadow.

Sitting inside of lonely jail cells, walking the cold streets at night, be chained up like an animal at my foster home, my pursuit of peace and happiness, my pride and belief that I can be somebody who utilizes my experiences to help others has carried me throughout the dark times. My desire to see better days continue to be my motivation to see another day. I will admit that I fantasize about the days when I'm successful in can look at those who mistreated me, and say "Look at me, now I am your creation."

For me, battling depression has been a daily task. I'm aware that to find true happiness, I must obtain inner peace. a critical element to this is accepting the past and utilizing those things that's happened to me to happen for me. Ex: If someone beat you up physically, until you accept that loss, you won't be at peace with yourself, not to mention the person whom you lost the fight to. Instead, you'll hold a grudge and spend countless amounts of time plotting your revenge. You may end up blaming yourself, doubting your own skills as a fighter. You wonder, how did you allow yourself to lose. Your pride takes a blow. You find it hard to be at peace with yourself, though you don't acknowledge it. But this is what happens, when you allow these types of thoughts to occupy your mind. Plus, you continue to give satisfaction to your opponent, by giving them your mind as a playground.

   For anyone who's dealing with depression, I recommend focusing on the process of accepting the issues that your depression derive from. Acceptance is the key. Have enough awareness of your self-worth to know that nothing is strong enough to keep you down as long as you are not willing to give up.

Anything that's been done is already history. And, history is a class in which we long to learn from in order to understand and build a better future. ......

Sitting in lonely jail cells, walking the cold streets at night, to being chained up like an animal at my foster home, my pursuit of peace and happiness, my pride and belief that I can be somebody who utilizes my experiences to help others has carried me throughout the darkest times. My desire to see better days continue to be my motivation to see another day. And, I'll admit that I fantasize about the days when I'm successful and can look at my haters and say, "Look at me now. I am your creation."

For me, battling depression has been a daily task. I'm aware that in order to find true happiness, I must first find inner peace. A critical element to this is accepting the past and using the things that happened to me to happen for me. Ex: If someone defeats you in a physical fight, until you accept that loss, you won't be at peace with yourself. And, therefore, you cannot even begin to build peace with the individual whom you lost the fight to. Instead, you'll hold a grudge, and spend countless amounts of time potting revenge. You may end up blaming yourself and doubting your abilities as a fighter.

You'd wonder, how'd you allow yourself to be beat? Are you not able to defend yourself? Your pride takes a shot.

Tears In A Jar

I stood outside, in the rain,

aside a puddle of mud.

Because, in that pile of dirt, I'd planted a seed, and that seed produced a rose, once the rain was done.

My tears fell. But, I caught them in a jar. Then, I placed the jar on my shelf, to stay forever.

They act as a memory of the bad times, which makes the better days undoubtedly so much better.

Scars on my wrist, from suicidal days. They'll never fade.

They represent my past hurt yet remind me of the pain I've overcame.

Standing in the rain, I smile, while holding my tears trapped in a jar. A road sign ahead of me reads, "Dead End". But, in the end, I know I've came so far.

A VICTIM OF BULLYING

Chapter #3

You never complain about the pain, because they say, "Words don't break bones".

Yet, the pain you feel is all too real…

Worse than sticks and stones.

Still, you smile, you never complain,

refusing to express that you're hurt

You pray, that tomorrow, others may simply realize what you're worth..

I Feel Your Pain.

Being Sincere...

I never listen to the sarcastic jokes they tell. Yet, I can't help but to hear them.

Knowing, I'll have to fight them all on my own, I can't help, but to fear them.

Out of all of the people to bother, what a coincidence, they've chosen me.

They say, "What don't kill you only makes you stronger,". Still, I've been feeling weak.

I never let them see me weep. For weeks, I've been holding back these tears.

Forcing a smile, all the while, if my tears were to shed, the world would consider them unreal.

But, this is real, so sincere. There's no façade... no lies.

Yet, at the same time, the truth is easy to hide, with so much on the line... my self-esteem... my joy... my life.

Looking for acceptance, steady losing the fight, it's hectic.

I smile at times, oppose to frowning. But the sight of my reflection, causes

emotional pain. This clownish smile is heavy. But it's my only protection

And, still I say, "This is real.. sincere.. no façade .. no lies."

Yet, in my mind, I struggle with knowing whether it's a lie.

Because, the truth is so easy to hide.

Solid

Sticks and stones may break my bones. But the words, I'll never feel.

I suppose a gang of bullies could beat me to death. But their words could never kill.

With no shame in my heart, nor any fear, I strive through life unrestricted…

Never allowing my enemies to deviate me from what I stand for, like a seasoned politician.

I'm living within the midst of my vision, being who I want to be.

I accept the things that I can't change, and the hate which will never cease.

Whatever don't kill's me will only make me stronger. So those who hate me… I love them more.

They help to make me better. The wind beneath my wings, they help me soar.

What was once my pain has become my pleasure, I've never felt so good.

Uniqueness is beautiful. It feels good to be misunderstood.

So yeah, sticks and stones may break my bones. But their words I'll never feel.

And, I suppose a gang of bullies could beat me to death. But their words could never kill.

WHEN YOU FEEL LIKE IT'S YOU AGAINST
The World

Chapter #4

You like by the saying, "trust no one". When you're down, they're nowhere to be found.

While everyone else seems to be moving up, this world is constantly dragging you down.

Alone in this world, when things go wrong, you have no choice but to take the blame.

Deemed guilty without a trial, expected to lose… dying to win… yeah…

I feel your pain.

    Awond.

Me against the world

It's me against this world. And along my side, I can't even See my shadow.

I woke up in the midst of War, I had no choice but to go to battle. My friends had promised me day would come along, But they were lying all along.

Now, It seems as if they've joined forces against me, falsely convincing me of being wrong.

I am mis understood by all, Nothing I do seems to be right. I woke, And the midst of A-war and the only take to be won or lost is my Life.

Who can I trust to trust. Anyone can be a spy.

I smile at them and they smile back, we're all meeting each other in disguise.   It's the odds are against me. But I'm left with no choice, but to go to battle.   Its me against the world, and along my side, I cant even see my shadow………. Poem, by Awond

Sacrifice...

It's no longer a secret, My pain is these haters pleasure. They love to know that their lives are better than mines. They pray that I never do better.

Regarding the statistics, I'm expected to lose, it'd be a surprise if I was to win the odds are against me, this game of chess has been rigged.

I'm simply a pawn in this game of life, a sacrifice, served on a platter. You could find the end of my story, within the start of my story. Sadly, my first chapter will be my last chapter.

I've been subjected to flagrant fouls, since the beginning of this game. Yet, no referee will ever blow its whistle.

Designed to lose, there's no potential for me to win, in the end. I'm unfortunately, simply caught up in the middle.   Poem, by Awond

My Testimony:

After spending many years on a path of self- destruction, I was finally at a point in my life where I saw potential for better days. at 17 I had just completed 2 years in juvenile Department Of Corrections. now after being out for a few months I have landed my first job ever working at Kmart. and I had just passed my GED test. my next plan was to go to college and take my life sort of more positive route. everything was going well until I violated my juvenile parole by driving without a license.

Now, I was back in juvenile serving a few months as a result of this violation. Fortunately, I only have 2 weeks left until I could get paroled and back to my plans of going to college and bettering myself. Well, at least that's what I had hoped for....

I Feel Your Pain

In the past, my current cell mate and I had a few minor altercations. but says I was focused on finishing might come in getting paroled I was more than willing to put the past behind me and avoid any confrontations with my cell mate. but with only 2 weeks left I received word that my cellmate had been secretly plotting an attack on me once we would be locked in our cell for the night.

At this point in my life I had more heart than brains. So, I wasted no time confronting my cell mate about these rumors. Full of bravado himself, my cellmate confirmed that the rumors were true. His response was, "It's either going to be you or me." Of course, all hell broke loose. We fought repeatedly, throughout the night and I wasn't losing.

After the fighting was done, I warned my cellmate that if he was to alert the guards to what had happened, he would have even more problems. I knew that if he was to tell, my chances of being paroled on time would be in jeopardy.

So, of course the next day, my cellmate took the first opportunity given to run to the guards and tell it all. Once they saw his face, there was little need to explain much more. Then, to make matters worse, the guy wanted to press charges against me. At this point, I was eligible to be tried as an adult. And, that's exactly what happened. With only a few weeks left before I was to be paroled, I was now being charged for assault and intimidation.

Once my girlfriend heard about the incident, she left me, thinking that I was going back to my old ways. DCFS quickly emancipated me, cutting off that source of support. 2 weeks ago, I was focused on getting out of juvie and going to college in now everything was going downhill.

I felt betrayed, misunderstood and as if I was being treated unfairly. I truly felt as if I had only been defending myself. I admit, I'd went overboard. But, when you're trapped in a cell with someone, and it's him or you... what's the limit to defending yourself. At

least, that's the way that I thought back then.
Despite what I felt, no one was siding with me. I felt as if it was me against the world. For once, I'd been optimistic about the future. But now I was back to believing that God intended for me to be the poster child for trouble and failure. Why me?

In the end, I pled guilty to intimindation {a class 4 felony}, in the hopes of receiving some county time and then moving on. But, of course, I never receive what I wish for out of life. So, why would things change now? Instead of some county time, I was sentenced to 2 years in prison. Two years in adult prison.

In the end, I ended up serving 6 months in prison. This put an end to my immediate plans for college. Instead, I ended up back on the road to self- destruction. Being that D.C.F.S had now emancipated me, I was released from prison with no support and a lot of animosity towards the world

Throughout life, I've learned that there will be times when the odds are against you. Things will go wrong, and others will not agree with your point of views. You will take losses. Yet, there is no better teacher than adversity. And, adversity is a part of life… the underlined thrive behind surviving. We all experience difficulties throughout life. Some deal with hardships better than others. Growing up, I wasn't one of these people.

The sun won't always shine. We cannot prevent the rain from coming. But we can control the way that we deal with the rain. Never let it drown you.

My philosophy is that I am my own master. I am in control of my own destiny. The fate of my future lies within my own hands… my own mind.

I'm an outlaw... a one man army, determined to survive against the odds. Wisdom... health... compassion for others... self-discipline... and education will assist me in my pursuit to achieve my goals. I will never surrender. These days, I'm committed to defeating any obstacle that may come my way, without self-destructing.

Today, the thought of the world being against me is not discouraging, it's actually motivating. Because, I know that I am my own master, and I have what it takes to prevail. So, now I embrace the moments when I feel as if the odds are against me, for this is when I can display my strengths and knowledge.

A Solid Solider... poem by Awond

Many people, rarely see a solid solider like me.
Often perceived as a statistic, many often overlook the key elements which makes me... me.
My birth alone was a problem, and I was born into this world that's full of many obstacles.
  I stay prepared to face the next negative situation, accepting the face that escaping adversity is a fantasy, if not completely impossible.

  I wonder, how aware of reality are those who classify me as cold hearted and egotistical, simply because I usually prefer to turn down love?
  When I do so, because in this cutthroat society, lust is often over-exaggerated, and when you're in need of support from those you trust, all of that momentarily love deteriorate, so instead you end up receiving none.

  I'm considered to have suicidal traits, because I see life when looking and the face of death.

But it is partly because I know my presence has been impactable enough to stay confined within the minds of many, when evil in the flesh there is nothing of me left.

People look at me aware that I'm the pathfinder for many. Then, they look away, confused by the person too deeply disguised to be seen.

and since a smile can be misconstrued as a sign of weakness I simply nod my head to this world, who have just seen something... someone who they may never again see... Mankind's and adversities greatest creation... a solid soldier like me

Committed.. poem by Awond

Propositioned as an opposition, this world has made me an outcast.
Solid like concrete, my beliefs, though contrary to others will forever... ever last.

I'm living, for what I'll die for... never deviating from my truth. In a world, where it's me against this world, I refuse to ever lose. Designed to be the solider on the front line, I wake up, ready for war. And, I'll take pride in being loyal to me... until this world and I depart

DEALING WITH DRUG ADDICTED PARENTS

Chapter # 5

In denial, your parents chasing that first high is something that you would rather not witness.

Open secrets, you never tell anyone else. Because even though, it'll help to talk about it, quite frankly, it's none of their business.

I feel your pain.

Josh... poem by, Awond

Little three old Josh stretches out his arms, as his mother walks through the door. He's hoping, she'll pick him up.

His mother notices him as she enters. But her mind is other stuff.

"Mommy!" he cries, following her to the couch. She pays the child no attention.

Josh's tears fall rapidly, as she wraps a belt around her arm. Too many times, has he saw this picture.

She sits back on the couch. Josh places his tiny hands on her knees, crying out, "Mommy, mommy, mommy." But he knows what's coming next. This daily routine started off as mommy's innocent hobby.

With the belt now fastened tightly around her arm, she takes a loaded needle from her pocket.
  Josh watches as she shoots the needles' substance into her fading vein.
Her eyeballs roll up into her eye sockets.

A daily thing. Josh assumes that's like usual him being ignored will shortly be over.
  Waiting, he watches as his moms' arm fall to her side and her head slumps down to her shoulder.
 Josh wait, understanding that he comes second, first mommy has to have her fix.
   But today, second will never come. Because mommy's overdosed and only 27, leaving 3 year old Josh waiting and watching… life's a bi###…………

My Testimony…

   To say that drugs tore my family apart would be an understatement. My parents drug addictions led to my siblings and myself being placed into the custody of Department and Children Family Services.
   I was only four years old, at the time. Yet, I vividly remember the night that the police barged into our home, snatching my two sisters, my younger brother and me up. I recall, the electricity being off and neither one of our parents being home. That night changed our lives forever.

   I've lived every day, feeling depressed and slightly ashamed about the fact that my parents were addicted to drugs. I was ashamed that I didn't have the ideal childhood. Their addictions ultimately led to me being placed in an abusive and neglectful foster home. Every day, I was praying, hoping that my parents would get clean, so that they could regain custody of us.
   As a child, it's not easy to understand addiction, nor accept

I Feel Your Pain

the reality that your parents are addicts. It's not a topic that one would easily discuss with their peers. It's even more difficult to deal with, when your every day life is impacted by it. And, for years to come, this would end up being my life.....

Leaning against the dresser in my mothers' bedroom, I breathed a sigh of relief. It was after 2A.M and it had been a long and exhausting night. It was now the dawn of Christmas Eve, and it was dawning on me that the wonderful Christmas I'd hoped for was on the verge of remaining a 13 year old fantasy, oppose to becoming a reality.

At 17 years old, I had not spent this holidays with my mother since I'd been took away from her when I was 4. and at this point I had only saw my mother maybe 10 times all for the past 13 years. Initially my mother had been opposed to the idea of me coming to her house for Christmas. I had been out of juvie for 4 and a half months after serving 2 years. All together Harry and I had not sought each other in over 3 years. Therefore, I did not care if she was against me visiting. Taking matters into my own hands I was determined to spend time with her. Ultimately that would be a bad idea.

After an awkward greeting, mom mother had left the house on 2 different occasions, making mysterious short trips somewhere. Bing that the weather was bad and it was past midnight at this point on her third trip I insisted that I ride along with her. Sadly to say she had been making trips to a local drug house. I did not know what was the right thing for me to do or say once I discovered this.

"Why are you staring at me like that?" My mother asked me,

After, catching me I heard a suspiciously. "What's wrong?"

I shrugged my shoulders. "I don't know," I responded. There was an awkward silence. "You see what you making me do?" She asked. Opening her hand, my mother showed me the 2 small crack rocks she'd apparently just bought. The yellowish white pebbles rested in her palm, symbolizing the source of 13 years of pain, separation, depression and so much more.

In the eyes of an observer I was unbothered, as I calmly stated, "That's something that a mother should never tell their child. Fortunately, I'm smart enough to not allow that to bother me."

Though that is what I'd said, in reality, I was deeply bothered by her statement. After being taken away from my parents, due to their addictions, only to go to a foster home and be subjected to extreme abuse, her words hit me like a double-edged sword. Even though, I knew that her statement was untrue, it was still tough to hear.

After a crazy night filled with attempting to physically keep my mother from getting high, her locking herself in the bathroom to do so anyways, crying and yelling, I ultimately ended up leaving town a few hours later, opting not to spend my Christmas day in chaos.

As of today, I assume that my mother is clean. I believe that my father does his best to stay clean. But, truthfully, I don't know. I don't see either of them enough to have that knowledge or to make any assumptions. For their own sake, I pray that they.

For years, I have dealt with being upset with my father for his drug addiction and the fact that me and my siblings have been impacted by it. It is hard to accept the possibility/reality that your parent is choosing to drugs opposed to being active in your life. I would not verbalize that's I felt hate and embarrassment regarding my parents because of their addictions. However, then reality is that this is true.

These days, I am wiser and more compassionate. I understand the seriousness of drug addiction. I sympathize with them to a degree. Just as I sympathize with anyone who is wasting in risking their life because of an addiction. Understanding that people make rational decisions when they're in their illness, I've been able to start the process of forgiving my parents, for some of the poor decisions they've made in the past. And, forgiving allows me to begin healing, emotionally. Nothing can make us stronger and wiser than experience itself.

After running away from home, I sold drugs and committed other crimes in order to get by. I spent a lot of time in the juvenile detention center, as a result of my criminal activities and the fact that I was refusing to return home. At 15 years old, I was sentenced to two years in the juvenile Department of Corrections. Throughout those two years, I watched other teenagers get support from their parents, while I never received a visit, a letter nor a dime from either of my parents. Two years of no family support or contact left me doing a lot of thinking and some soul searching.

It dawned on me that while I was selling crack cocaine to people, I was contributing to the same destruction that had initially destroyed my life, up until that moment. While I hated the thought of someone selling my parents drugs, I was selling drugs to someone else's parents. Perhaps, somewhere, there were a kid hating me. At that moment, I told myself that I was done selling crack. But I admit, I wasn't committing to becoming a saint.

Being the child of drug addicted parents, one has the privilege to break the cycle. It's ultimately a gift and a cursed. I'm choosing to make the best of the gift and break the curse.

Ashore... a poem, by Awond.

Drowning in your sorrows, drowning in that bottle, I wonder how much of you has washed away as well.

I felt myself, being washed away with you. Yet, I refuse to allow my boat to cease to sail.

Now, I've made it ashore. But I left a life jacket and a raft, which I pray you utilize.

It hurts me, to see you skelp away from help, but this time, it's not my objective to scrutinize.

I emerged from that cloud of smoke... which was once lingering between us.

They say, "The apple does not fall far from the tree." I pray that this don't mean us.

I trust and pray that tomorrow, destiny lessens thee sorrows, you feel obligated to drown.

But one of us must live to tell the tale. So, I can't allow your addiction to drag me down.

I'll catch your tears, whenever you're in reach. You should kill the distance.

I stand on this side of the cloud of smoke, because the sight on the other side is too harsh for me to continue to witness.

Trapped in your cloudy world, I sense that there is love at the core And, for as long as we live, I have love to give, just incase you float safe ashore. poem, by Awond.

CONTEMPLATING SUICIDE

Chapter #6

You believe then dying must be easier than living because this life is more like death.
 Pain, fear and regret… the weight of the world gets heavier on your shoulders with every breath. I feel your pain.

So Ready To Die… a poem, by Awond

 I said quiet at times deep in thought impatiently counting the seconds to minutes the days,
 Wondering how much longer will it take for this lonely and miserable life to fade away.
 Suicide is now my enemy for constantly turning its back on me you see I gave in to the power of suicide but suicide slipped from the power of me.
  Life has done me wrong since day one, showering me with pain obstacles in sorrow.
  Marvel is supposed to be a better day but like yesterday, today I have no desire to see tomorrow.

so when Death arrives, with its stride, looking for its next victims face,
If that person believes that it is not their time to die I will gladly take their place.

I do not have any bags packed I will rather leave all that I know of this world behind.
and to you who stole my heart you can keep it because without it I will be fine.
oh Lord ... Lord may not open his gates and embrace a depressing little old sinner like me. But even if Hell is where I am heading I'll quickly leave this world of no peace and take my chances with the beast.

Silent Surrender

I smile, but any wise man can tell,
 I wear the smile of a pretender.
From anyone's perspective, I appear eager to live life.
Yet, on the inside, I'm ready to surrender.

Spending days, plotting upon ways to end this pain, I'm preparing to leave this world behind.
And, sometimes it's hard to say "goodbye", yet somedays it's harder to stay alive.

All of the time, I long for times, when I'm not drowning in my depression.
Feeling neglected, amongst my list of reasons is the intention to teach a lesson.

A lesson... to those, who intentionally left me deserted, in the dark, tending to my broken heart.
A lesson; to them who act as if their words could never leave scars.

Spending days, plotting ways to end this pain, I've checked the price for a ticket on the next flight heading to the afterlife.

You see, some people fear death. But I can't imagine anything being... after life.

I never share these thoughts. Because, these are things that others won't understand.

Besides, then they'll make plans to kill my plans. And, I refuse to lose and die at the hands of another man.

So, I smile, but any wise man can tell that I'm wearing the smile of a pretender.

On the outside, I appear ready to see what tomorrow has in store. But on the inside, I'm ready to surrender.

My Testimony...

Going up in an abusive foster home not fitting in with my peers suffering from low self-esteem, These, were just some of the reasons that I often dreaded seeing another day. Convinced that's my life was never going to get any better I have spent many days contemplating suicide. I looked at death as an escape, as if it was my pain reliever.

in the eyes of the world I gave a great facade pretending their life was well. In reality I was trapped in hell. exhausted from trying to survive I've always took advantage of the effortless act of flashing a small to disguise my pain.

but no matter how good I was at fooling others I could never fool myself. I lived with the truth against my will. and with every day that went by I felt more alone isolated in the world that was cold and lonely. I felt as if I was being pushed to the edge I desperately started seeking relief.

I woke up, still exhausted after having had another sleepless night. I had managed to doze off for a short amount of town before the sound of the basement door being unlocked and open woke me up. my entire body ached, as I struggled to stand from my kneeling position. With my hands duct taped behind my back and wrapped around a pole, standing was no easy task. but the sound of my foster mother coming gave me the strength that it took. fear set into my heart as my foster mother me, a sinister look was in her eyes.

Furious about the fact that I had ran away a few days ago my foster mother had gave me a vicious beat down once the police had caught me and returned me to her custody. I had told the cops that's my foster mother was abusive which is why I had ran away. but after speaking with her they had took her words over mines. Immediately after the police had left my foster mother Forced me to the basement save my hands behind my back after stripping me naked and then, beat me with a broomstick until it broke until several pieces. Now my body was bruised and aching from head to toe.

my naked body shivered from both the cold breeze sweeping through the basement and fear smiling my foster mother berated me about my failed attempt to run away. see promised me that I would never be able to have the cops believe me over her. I admit that's for the last 8 years of my life she had been correct about this.

my foster mother assured me that she would Kill me before she would ever allow me to get her into any trouble. after already being found guilty of abuse neglect and torture and the case of my oldest sister my foster mother was determined to not have any more charges brought against her.

she assured me that if I kept running away she would kill me and hide my body someplace where it's would never be found. believing that's my future would be full of the same abusive and harsh experiences I had already endured, I silently prayed for God to just let me die. My desire to live was completely gone. I was trapped, literally.

When you spend many hours isolated in a basement you have a lot of time to think. within that time I came up with the philosophy that if I'm not scared to death, I should not be scared to live. doing my darkest days it was hard to be optimistic. occasionally I still have these days. but I have the courage to face another day and keep going. depression is a deadly disease which leads people to self-destruct. I battle with depression even now every day. and I often consider calling it quits.

but At the same time, I believe that I am working of being alive. I know that I am someone who deserves to live this life that I have been given. so I continue to give myself that opportunity. Part of the reason is because I feel the need to prove that I am stronger than any obstacle standing in front of me or anything that I have had to endure.

It's a natural human impulse to try to survive. No one will fall into an ocean and not attempt to swim to safety, even those who want to drown. So, you'll kick and stroke away.

The only guarantee that life will give us is the fact that we all will die. So, there's no reason to wish for, nor chase it. It'll be here. In the meantime, we must try to live the best life possible.

Many people considered pride to be a self- destructive and selfish characteristic for anyone to have and display. However, I am confident that if I did not have a strong sense of pride, I would have Follow through on my suicidal plans many years ago.

chained up like an animal in my foster home, sleeping on park benches at a young age, growing up in jail cells, being rejected, misunderstood and ignored by certain family members and peers, I never truly stopped believing that I'm worth something, that I'm someone of importance, or that my life here on this earth has meaning. As I write this very sentence, it dawns on me that I never stopped loving myself. While I was all I ever had in others were doing me wrong, I believed in myself and my optimism was always stronger than my pessimism. with No Fear of dying I've stopped being afraid to live.

to anyone contemplating suicide I simply say, "Be brave. Breathe easy. Go to sleep and wake up to a better day and be a better person. Remember, it will never rain forever."
written by, Awond

My Brother... a poem, by Awond

My brother, where you are, I've been. And, to wherever you're going, I'm either there, or that's where I'm heading.
With a contradictive vision of where I wish to be, I travel through life, exploring all directions.

My brother, I feel your pain. When you're injured, I'm hurting inside.
My tears no longer flow, though. So, instead, when you cry, I cry.

That painful song which your heart sings happen to be a song that I know too well.
In this rumored to be 'Land Of The Free', where they ask, "Why do the caged birds sing?", With you, I hope to see heaven, after this hell.
In this world, where you're nobody until you've become to be somebody on top,
I've acknowledged your presence, even when others thought that you were no one worthy to watch.

I understand, the reasons that you do the things that you do. When you struggle, trust me, I sympathize with you.
Where you are, I've been. When you cry, I cry. And, through pain,

I Feel Your Pain

I helped written that sad song that you sing. It's true. My brother, I'm with you....

More Than Life... poem, by Awond.

I'm an undiscovered treasure, the pot of gold at the rainbow, which most believe this world will never find.

   A motherless son, a chilling blaze.. in the flesh, I'm a wise thought, seeking the shelter of a mind.

   I see those tears that's too old to show, on the faces of those who silently suffer.
 If I was to ever swallow my pride, pride would surely be my last supper.

   I've realized that I'm the light to light in this dark world. Yet, no one's brave enough to flip my switch.
   My words are the key to heal this world. Give me your broken heart. I promise to return it fixed.

      After I build you up, if you fall apart, I'll simply build you up again.

No longer living to die, I'm dying to live. As the day ends, my journey begins.

   When it comes to defeating obstacles, I've overcame that final step.
I'm a helping hand, when needed. However, most people are too proud to ask for help.

   I've been sitting back, keeping track of everything that God's been making.
First, he impressed us with light, then with life. And, now I'm Gods' greatest creation....... Amen

NO ONE TO TRUST.

Chapter #7

Friends leave you stranded,
  deserted in a cutthroat land.
After all the promises you've been given,
  you can't even find a helping hand.

  Some say, "Blood is thicker than water."
But, at times, that's hard to believe.
Because no one appears to be trustworthy.
You can't even trust the blood that you bleed.

Dinner, With Judas… a poem, by Awond

    I'd set up the dinner table for two, anticipating the company of a friend.
A well planned meal awaited us, along with a few drinks, intended before the night would end.
  We had things to discuss, such as the plans for tomorrow, as well as the future for us all.
  If we were ever trees in this world, our support and trust for one another would be the ground, catching us, if we were to ever fall.
   My friend finally arrived, dinner was served, we ate, while whispering about our plans.
  Aware that if our words landed upon the wrong ears, this would

be our last dance.

A change was coming, delivered by us. This was set to be a change that would benefit us all.

Of course certain individuals opposed of this change, and these individuals were on the prowl.

With dinner served and ate, we shared glasses of wine, trying to ignore the danger that we were in. It was us against the world. It felt good to have a friend.

A few glasses of wine later, my friend decided, it was time for him to go about his way.

We made plans to reunite the following day, aware that it was the big day.

The day which our plans would fail or succeed. Secret intentions would be put to the test.

With our last secret supper complete, my friend left. and I decided to rest.

No more than a few minutes later, there was a knock on my door I quickly prayed that my friend hadn't changed his mind.

After months of planning… whispering about bringing justice to others, tomorrow was set to be our time.

Opening the door, I was caught off guard, seeing an army of oppositions. For just a split second….

I was startled and confused, no doubt clueless.

Then as I was snatched up and carried away to be lynched, it dawned on me,

I'd just had dinner with Judas.

No Love. No Trust. A poem, by Awond

Confident my heart will be broken if I was to ever give it to someone I hold onto my heart tightly into the day that I die.

Unable to find anyone who I can trust to love I suppose it'll always be me, myself and I.

In this cutthroat society, I trust no one, because smiles are often hiding sinister grins, all the while.

People will applaud you, when you win, in public. Then, behind closed doors, they plot to bring you down.

Once upon a time, I was a fool, just as Adam was, when he trusted Eve. But, never again, will I be.

Because, promises are like a ship that's badly built, carrying you out to shore, it's designed for you to sink.

So, I willingly swim within the midst of these sharks, aware of what I'm up against.

Because, I'll rather die alone, oppose to with others, who's words of love and trust have hints of mince.

I don't depend on anyone. Because anybody can have a change of mind.

I only believe what I can see. In regards to love and trust, this world has left me blind.

They say, "Keep your friends close and your enemies closer." So, I prefer moving in the dark, while it's hard to see.

Because in the light, I can see my shadow lurking. And, I don't trust anyone who's trying to get close to me.

My Testimony...

My foster mother was a master manipulator. While she was torturing my siblings and myself behind closed doors, to the public, she was presenting herself as a compassionate, God fearing, law abiding individual.

On Saturdays, she would beat, starve and chain me in the basement. Then, on Sunday, she would dress us up and parade us through church, where she was an active member. Our neighbors and my foster mothers' associates had bought into her façade. If I could've told them the true horror she imposed on my siblings and me, no one would've believed me. My foster was too good of an actress.

My foster mother's behavior had a huge impact on the way that I looked at others. She left me skeptical about others, who try to portray themselves as sincere and compassionate. Nowadays, when I encounter people like this, I always question their motives....

When D.C.F.S removed my oldest sister from the household due to abuse, I risked my safety, by corroborating the allegations against my foster mother. I'd told the truth, hopeful and confident that they'd take me away as well. Instead, I was placed back in the same foster home, left to defend for myself, at just nine years old. From that moment on, my faith in the system was gone. I no longer trusted authorities.

Witnessing how so- called friends will utilize your darkest secrets against you in a moment of anger, I could never trust them with my reality. Going throughout life trusting no one made me feel as if I was in a world of my own. Considering everyone to be untrustworthy, I was paranoid in started to think everyone was out to take advantage of me. I had begun to despise people, even before I ever met them ...

Many people say, "Blood is thicker than water." And, despite having little contact with my blood relatives due to me being adopted, I was so hurt by the abuse I was suffering in my foster home, I quickly embraced that theory.

For years, while being tortured mentally and physically by my foster mother, I'd been convinced that my life would've been much better, if I could reconnect and live with my real relatives. I was also convinced that if my blood relatives new of what's my foster mother was putting my siblings and myself through my foster mother would be in some real trouble, perhaps even and some danger.

Then when I was 13 years old, I received some of the worst news I will ever hear in my life. wow I was on the run in staying with my mother for the first time since I was 4 years old, I'd told her, "I want to meet my real family." I was eager to meet cousins, aunts, uncles, everyone. I told her, I wanted to meet my grandmother on both sides of my family.

"Well, you already know your grandma from my side of the family," My mother responded. "How could that be?" I'd asked.
"That's the woman you've been staying with." My mothers' words hit me like a ton of bricks. My heart was instantly broken, as I took in my mothers' words. My foster mother was really my mothers' mom? I cried.

Too busy beating and starving us, my foster parent apparently had forgot to inform us that we were her grandchildren. To say that I was shocked would be an understatement. This news was worst than a slap in the face. Every, since that moment, I no longer believed that blood is thicker than water.

Trust people at your own risk! But most importantly, trust yourself. There's no one on this earth who has the capability to do more to or for you than you're capable of doing to and for yourself. People will deceive and let you down. The best thing that you can do is be the best person possible for yourself......

MY MIND... MY HEART. A
Poem, by Awond

My heart has been repeatedly broken while my thoughts have led me in the wrong direction.
so it's only wise for me to develop a plan that will provide me with some sense of protection.
now my heart is my mind the feelings I feel are only thoughts, slight beliefs.

love at first sight is a possibility if I believe that it is love I see with these eyes.
if all goes wrong and I am betrayed I can change my love to hate with only a change of mind.

The average heart is vulnerable, uneducated, too weak and easy to be misled.
So to prevent reliving a broken heart I think that I love, instead.

By the power of my mind, I feel. So, if whatever I think I feel for some reason be forced to change...
By thought, I can replace my feelings. Oh yes, a mind is a terrible thing to waste.

My heart only thinks that I love. It only thinks that I hate. I cannot be hurt or misled any longer.
No pain... no sorrow... no tears. My heart is my mind and vice a versa.

Sincerely, Awond.

My Better Half... A Poem, By Awond

My friend, my brother, my better half, it hurts me so deeply to see you in pain.
I feel as if I have been defeated, watching you suffer lost after lost, when you only wish to gain.

Time after time, you are taken advantage of, by those who you trust to trust.
how many times must I heal your broken heart and remind you that in this world there is no justice, there is just us?

My friend, I will forever be with you, catching the deceitful signs but you seem to miss...
those frowns painted with smiles the wish for death hidden in the mist of that sweet kiss.

It upsets me, to watch you be seduced by those whose intention is to see you weaker.
But, I'll always be there to carry you along. I truly am my brothers' keeper.

But still I say, "Shame on you, for forcing to contribute to be your worst enemy."
I've been dying to hand you the key to your dreams. Yet you force me to keep it within me, until the end of me.

My friend, my brother, my better half, if only you would listen, you could save us both.
Acknowledge my presence, utilize my weapon. My determination could keep us afloat.
Leave those who mislead you, the materialistic addictions and

the past times which confines you.
   Face me, see what I see, life through your eyes, reflected from my eyes. Here, stands all you'll ever need, it's true.
Because, you are I and I am you

BEING YOUR OWN WORST ENEMY

Chapter # 8

Your objective is to make thing right. Yet, somehow you do things all wrong... Procrastinating, when it's time to stand up is the only reason you've been down so long. Usually, it takes no time to identify who is blocking you from making your next move... But, identifying that person is difficult to do, when the person to blame is you..   I Feel Your Pain

..A Letter to You, From Me..

Dear You, This a letter written with intentions to know you, and understand, how you feel about me... My love for you grows everyday. But I believe your love for me occasionally get weak. Against my wishes, you control me. And, the things you do make this truth hard to swallow...   You step eagerly into negative situations, in doing so, you drag me along, also. I've been by your side all my life and initially, I didn't think my loyalty would be a problem... We've plotted to rise to the top. Unfortunately, you're keeping us at the bottom. I've faced many obstacles, because of you. Remember, your actions landed us in jail? Unfortunately, you're in control of me and you're making this one life we have hell.

Often, you become suicidal, and I know you're only thoughts away from killing yourself...You live, I live, when you die, I'll die but I'd like to avoid meeting an early death. I pray that you make better choices. You should be tired of fighting battles... If you don't do it for you, do it for me, At the least, think about it.   Sincerely Yours,   Your Shadow

Loyal Passenger..

Full of rage and thoughts of revenge, it's a challenge to make rational decisions... I shake my head, observing, the inside, from outside, I'm stuck in an awkward position. Watching myself, blind with fury, at any moment, I may self-destruct... I see myself drowning with hate and I wonder, have I ever known love? I thrall, due to my own actions, an actual self-kept prisoner, intellectually and morally...Your selfish to seek help or admit defeat, I'm silently drowning in the sea of sorrows that   I personally bestowed in me. Singing on a sinking ship my life resembles scenes from the movie 'Titanic.' I sense death awaits me, yet I never ever change my route and pledge to never panic. My own best friend.my own worst enemy. I'm a loyal passenger promising to finish this trip... Shackled to myself, for better or worse, singing on this sinking ship.

..My Testimony..

I was 17 and preparing to go to college, within a matter of months. I'd stayed focused, over the last five months, working my first job and getting my G.E.D. Being humble and wise was getting me closer to my goals, until one night. I was in Quincy, Illinois with my girlfriend (Crystal) and some of her friends. The girls revealed that they'd never been to East Saint Louis but would like to go. I'm originally from East Saint Louis and told them, I'd take them and show them around. Well they wanted to go, now. So, despite the fact that I was on juvenile parole and despite the fact that I didn't have a drivers' license, the four of us piled into a Chevy Caprice and hit the road, heading to East Saint, nearly two hours away.

Only when we arrived, did I wonder, 'What are we going to do?' It was about 2 a.m. With nothing to do, I paid a quick surprise visit to my cousin (Carletta), before taking the girls on a ride around town... Crystal asked me to slow down as I was driving way beyond the speed limit. Laughing I told her," Just put your seat belt on." Telling her that would turn out to be the best thing I'd done all night. Minutes later, I was coming down a road, doing about 65 mph. Only when I got several feet from the end of the street did I realize that I was on a T. Bird road. Now I wish I'd took Crystals' advice. I attempted to make a sharp left turn, hoping to avoid a disastrous situation. But I'd have no such luck. The Chevy Caprice flew across the street, hopped the curb and crashed into someone's house, knocking a portion of the wall down. The air bags popping out upon impact was probably, the only thing that saved us from being thrown from the car. Plus, we had our seat belts on. Crystal pulled me from the car. She had a fractured jaw and a broken thumb. I was coughing up blood. I was a fool.... This incident landed me back in juvenile. I lost my job, of course. My plans to go to college where out the window. And, Crystal who I'd been infatuated with ever since I was 14, she moved on. And I could only blame myself. **** Once, someone casually asked me," Are you your own best friend?" And maybe giving the question more thought than I was expected to, I responded, "No. I wouldn't expect my best friend to subject me to the things that I was subjecting myself to." Ever since that moment focus of being my own best friend. Of course, I'm human and making mistakes is a part of living and learning. And I still continue to live and learn till this day. But I do a better job at looking out for my own best friend, while trying to be my own best friend.... When ones' material items are gone, and the people who's support to be your support system has disappeared (for whatever reason). The only thing we'll have left in this world is ourselves. So when and if that time comes, it's best to be working for you, oppose to against you. We are our own best asset. Even when we bring adversity onto ourselves, we are the only ones that can see to it that we over come it. When all you have is yourself, it's best to be with your own best friend, oppose to your own worst enemy. Make rational decisions. Love thyself..

..The Man..

The man is my enemy, his only intentions are to destroy me and keep me down...When I think he's out of plans to ruin my life, he thinks of a new plan, somehow...From my birth, he's killed my self esteem, telling me," You're black, in a world where black is ugly.", "I didn't ask to be black," I'd respond. Then he'll say ,"Still, you're black and ugly." 'The Man' installed a hatred for school ,in me, yet simultaneously, a strong love for wealth..."The school system will fail you," he said. "You'd be better of if you just quitted yourself," Whenever I thought of getting a job, while knowing that Caucasians were trying to get it.. As soon as the thought entered my mind, 'The Man' whispered, "Think realistic,"... "In this white mans' world, blacks shall get no peace, no president, no glory... No break...a bogus case, and no chance at a happily ending story." 'The Man' installed a slight shame in my mind and a hate in my heart, for me simply being me... So I decided to find 'The Man' with the plan to understand what the problem could be. Never to my knowledge had I saw 'The Man' and I couldn't find him now... No matter which direction I looked, 'The Man' was not around. Now I couldn't see him and his disrespectful comments I couldn't hear... After all these years of toughness, could it be? 'The Man' had hid in fear? Forever he'd known my thoughts, if they were constructive, he'd break them down...yet, when they were self destructive, he'd encourage me to carry them out. But, now 'The Man' who'd been so tough ,was hiding, not evenspeaking... "Could it be?" I asked myself. "After all these years, have I beat him?". Later I was thinking about 'The Man' who I'd always heard, yet never seen...it was then, I had epiphany.. 'The Man' had always been inside of me!   Now today I know, whether a man is white or black, for him to stop me from succeeding he'll need some help... Because no man can do more to, or for me than I've ever done to and for myself..   p.s. ...We are 'The Man'

Intuition...

Through these eyes, I see, The best route for me to travel...These hands have held the weight of life at times...and, it's never been too much to handle. These feet have been too much to handle. These feet have traveled, a million miles, from hell and back, again and again... My heart has craved righteous deeds, white my mind has plotted on sin. Alive, but not living.. adversity can bring an end to a mans patience...I'll die to be alive, yet I'm stronger than the old me, and my thoughts of surrendering now surrender to the power of my tenacity and invigoration.. with little hesitation..

I've traveled the wrong way, down a one-way lane, without a map or any protection...Still I trust myself to look out for my best interest and guide me in the direction. Because though advise us to go North or South...Only through these eyes, do I see the best route.

TRYING TO FIND YOURSELF

Chapter 9

You question who you are. But more importantly who're you meant to be? You sense that the real you is locked away, begging to be set free. But, where in the world is the key? You're soul searching, in the dark... And all the time, the thoughts in your mind challenges the desires in your heart..

.. My Worth..

Yesterday morning, I studied the Bible, but I spent the night doing the Devil's work...only half as righteous as I wish to be I wonder, how god will value my worth. They say, "I'm as much of a son as God as anyone,". Yet, I was born in this hell hole...If I could, I would carry this world to better days. But in the midst of saving myself, how much weight can my hands? When you know better, you should do better, so I feel slightly, guilty, when I do wrong.. I'm suicidal, yet so vital I'm so weak, yet so strong mixed, like I'm mulatto People always ask me what I am.. I smile because it's the polite thing to do but, this smile is part of a scam. Tomorrow morning, I'm scheduled to study the Bible, but tomorrow night I'll be doing the Devil's work. I admit I'm only half of righteous as I'd like to be, how god would   Value my worth.

..Who Am I..

I often stare at myself in the mirror, each time, growing more curious about the person I see…Though, it's the familiar face I've saw for years, I feel as if there's a stranger hiding underneath.

Eager to make an appearance and wash my memories of this familiar face away….These feelings grow and show, through the eye of my familiar face, everyday. I've grown to hate the person that I see staring at me, from the opposite side of the mirror … The fact that he's not me and I'm not him is suddenly so much clearer. I wonder, who hides beneath this flesh I can hear I'm screaming to be set free.. A hidden slave, imprisoned by my own skin, why can't I just let me be me? Don't hate me, hate him, for the awful things you've witnessed me do.. He hates me and I hate him. So if you hate me, I'm with you. Who am I, I ask myself, while staring through the eyes of the stranger in the mirror… I feel relieved, as tears escape from his eyes, and I embrace the reality that I'm not him and he's not me…suddenly, it's so much clearer.

..My Testimony..

When I was 14, I had to complete an outpatient drug program (for smoking weed). During these sessions, I would share my poetry. My counselor at the center took a liking to my poetry, taught me how to type it and save it on a computer disk. I've been writing, poetry, etc. ever since I was six years old. So I've always been aware of the power of words and how intricate my writings could be. Yet, I was caught off guard, by the fact that my counselor understood and argued with some of the view I'd expressed within my poetry. She thought I might have a true talent and some wisdom. Most importantly, she believed that my poetry could be helpful to others. And, that meant a lot to me. I'd never felt valued before. But within time I quickly started to feel uneasy. Having my counselor share my thoughts and my feelings and believe in me was too much. All my life, I'd wanted to be a helpful hand to others…something like a motivational speaker, while being accepted and understood. The fact that my counselor knew things I'd never shared before bothered me. While I wanted to be a "good guy" I believed that the previous 5 years I'd spent "wilding" in the streets and going in and out of juvenile had made that impossible. I'd often remind my counselor that I'd just don't two years in juvenile and was a "street guy". Who I thought I was wasn't the person I wanted to be. At 17 I was having an identity crisis, I was not the person who I truly believed I was meant to be. But I felt like I couldn't change now. I'd been portraying myself as a thug, and I'd bought into it myself.'

****

One day my younger sister Alexis came to visit me in prison. At this point, I hadn't saw her in over 10 years and felt that she might look at me as the brother she once know, initially, only to be disappointed of crimes I'd committed my gang involvement, etc. So minutes into the visit, I warned her, " I'm not the little boy that I use to be."

Alexis adamantly disagreed with me saying, "You're still the same. You haven't changed at all." Hearing her say that made my heart smile. It felt good, to feel someone recognize me as who I truly was. From the moment that I ran away (for good) at 12 years old, I'd done my best to distance myself from the victim I'd been while I was living in my foster home. And, I admit, in the process, I lost sight of who I truly was.

****

I'm not meant to be, who I'm expected to be, This realization has helped me not allow my circumstances to dictate who I am as an individual. Trying to be the person that others expect us to be often distance us from who we're meant to be. Adopting society's beliefs and embracing others perception of me has occasionally deviated me from the path I feel I'm destined to travel. Who I'm expected to be is not the man I'm destined to be.... Never let others tell you who you are.

..Stereotypical..

Living in a crime infested environment, outsiders peek in and see me as a career criminal. The way that I define myself, verbally, society disregards as being trivial. My pears seminal perspectives tell them, who they believe I should be. Confined within their imagination, I've often forgot about the person that I could be. Stereo typed, I'm losing this fight, and losing myself in the process. Initially, I was convinced that I was more than average, then society convinced me that I'm much less. This world is a kleptomaniac, Stealing my identity... Forcing me to live life as a disciple, But I'm meant to be an entity... My race, my past, and my environment, these things seem to interest most people. So bombarded with the stereotypes, I've grown close with them without them I feel feeble. Inside this crime infested environment, outsiders peek in and see me as a career criminal. And even though I know I'm much more trying to convince them of this seems so trivial. To portray someone, me being that someone, as someone other than who this world claim I am can be quite critical. It's much safer to hide inside this disguise and, unfortunately, that's quite typical. So for my faith to my name I've changed everything. Nothing remains the same.. And I vow to never be the same.. confined in a cage..

..I Found Someone.. With no one who I trusted to trust and no who I loved to love.. Suited for death like a gurney, I started the painstaking journey to discover who my special   someone was. With loneliness lurking me, adversity begged me to deviate from my course.. In return I'll find someone.. not that special someone.. instead someone who falls short... I turned down the momentarily smiles, knowing all the while, I'd find someone better... But I'll be lying if I said during hopeless times I didn't write and then sign love and then sign suicide letters. But just as nature was drying the ink and my abused and misused heart ship started to sink. I found someone who's strong enough to carry me along, during times when I feel weak. Someone who I'd never considered because I was always looking to others. Though I pushed behind this someone emerged to the front of the line using all strength this individual could muster. I found someone who loves me, for me, and until my death they'll offer me help. I found someone special.. a true friend, throughout this journey, I found myself.

I choose to share the information in this book with the hopes that someone could benefit and be inspired by it. Most of these personal testimonies I've chose to kept private up until this moment.

Even to this day, I'm hesitant to discuss certain issues. However; I believe that we all go through adversity and the ones who survive and gain knowledge from such tribulations have been chosen to do so, with the main purpose of using their experiences and knowledge to help others going through similar experiences. When I say "I Feel Your Pain", it's sincere. I chose to share my testimonies as a sign of my sincerity. At this point, my hopes are that aside from helping others, others may have the strength overcome through own trials and tribulations, gain knowledge and wisdom from them and ultimately help others to do the same.

I want to thank a few people for helping me stay focused and motivated throughout my life, and for simply listening at times when an open ear was needed. BRENDA JONES: my auntie who's always been like a mother figure... words can't explain. My siblings, Alexis, Davion, and Angelica. If anyone knows my pain to the fullest it's them. KELLY Renne Clary, who I call my god Mom. Crystal I, am old friend, who my love for literally kept my striving to see another day at times. Tara K, always been a friend and supporter. Jeri Santana... always my sister. All of my childhood friends that helped me out during times. Joi H... you held me down at times, it's all love. Many more names I can call out. Last but not the least,

Shanna. Thanks for helping me get this book ready to upload. Ima simply say it's all love. Hopefully I can pay you back in time. Appreciate the patience.